P9-CED-326

SEXUALLY TRANSMITTED DISEASES

Elaine Landau

ENSLOW PUBLISHERS, INC.

Bloy St. & Ramsey Ave.   P.O. Box 38
Box 777   Aldershot
Hillside, N.J. 07205   Hants GU12 6BP
U S A   U K

DRAWINGS BY HERMELIE HEIMLICH

Copyright © 1986 by Elaine Landau

Library of Congress Cataloging in Publication Data

Landau, Elaine.
  Sexually transmitted diseases.

  Bibliography: p.
  Includes index.
  Summary: Describes the characteristics, symptoms, diagnosis, and treatment of venereal diseases and infections.
  1. Venereal diseases—Juvenile literature. [1. Venereal diseases] I. Title.
RC200.2.L35   1986   616.9'5   85-4349
ISBN 0-89490-115-X

Printed in the United States of America

10 9 8 7 6 5 4 3 2 1

CONTENTS

For some outstanding young adult librarians at The New York Public Library for their generous help and guidance in my creations:

Ruth Rausen—Coordinator, Young Adult Services
Beryl Eber
Bonnie Goldstein

FOREWORD

The time for young people to learn about sexually transmitted diseases is before their first sexual experience. Many schools in the United States have a course in family living and human sexuality; all should. The course should include sexually transmitted diseases (STDs).

This book presents factual information about STDs. It is written clearly and in a straightforward manner without attempting to unduly scare the reader. Sexually transmitted diseases, however, *should* be a cause for concern. They can cause disfigurement, sterility, and even death.

There are ways to prevent these diseases and to stop their spread. The author presents these methods in plain language while stressing early diagnosis and treatment. These messages should reach young people and be heeded.

Donald Armstrong, M.D.

Chief, Infectious Disease Service
Director, Microbiology Laboratory
Memorial Sloan-Kettering Cancer Center

Professor of Medicine
Cornell University Medical College

PREFACE

For most of recorded history, sexually transmitted diseases have accounted for a large proportion of all deaths, disability, human misery, and economic loss due to illness. Prevention and control of these diseases have always been hampered by the limits that Western societies have placed on the study and discussion of sex and sexuality. The "sexual revolution" has contributed to the current epidemic of sexually transmitted diseases, but also has fostered changes in attitudes that have made it easier to control them and to educate the public about them. This book is a manifestation of these changes.

Most sexually transmitted diseases have a far greater impact on women than on men, although responsibility for spreading them falls equally upon both. The majority of these infections cause more subtle symptoms in women, leading to delays in seeking medical attention. They are harder to diagnose in women than in men, and women are much more likely to suffer serious consequences.

The risk of sexually transmitted diseases and their complications is greatest in sexually active young people. Thus, the ones at highest risk are those with the least awareness of the medical, psychological, and social consequences of careless sexual behavior and the least knowledge about prevention of these consequences. According to some estimates, fifty percent or more of young adults will acquire a sexually transmitted infection before age thirty-five.

There can be no doubt that knowledge is a potent and necessary weapon against the threat of sexually transmitted diseases. In the absence of knowledge, stern advice to limit sexual activity has little effect.

This book is written to help anyone who reads it make a responsible, informed choice about his or her sexual practices. The parent, counselor, or teacher who discusses it with a young person will be making a tangible investment in that person's health and happiness.

H. Hunter Handsfield, M.D.

Director, Sexually Transmitted Disease
 Control Program
Seattle-King County Department of Public Health

Associate Professor of Medicine
University of Washington School of Medicine

A WORD ABOUT
SEXUALLY TRANSMITTED DISEASES

Sexually transmitted diseases (STDs) are epidemic in the United States and Canada today. Each year over ten million new cases arise. As a result, anyone who is currently sexually active is at greater risk than ever before of contracting a sexually transmitted disease.

There are a number of reasons for the marked increase and spread of these diseases, which were formerly grouped under the name venereal diseases (VD). The last two decades have witnessed a dramatic shift in sexual values. Many people have developed a new, freer sense of morality, resulting in a greater number of sexual contacts per person as well as an overall increase in sexual relations. In addition, as sexual practices and techniques become more varied, infections once confined to either the mouth or the genitals are now spread to different parts of the body.

Contraceptive modes have also influenced the spread of sexually transmitted diseases. Previously, barrier methods such as the condom and diaphragm were the most commonly used forms of birth control. In addition to preventing pregnancy, these barrier methods also provided some protection against contracting a disease transmitted sexually.

Modern preferred methods of birth control do not offer such protection. It has been found recently that using an IUD (intrauterine device) or the Pill for contraception may actually render a woman more susceptible to some sexually transmitted diseases. Some researchers believe that use of the Pill causes certain changes in body chemistry which alter the acid/alkaline balance or pH level of the vagina, thereby creating a more conducive environment for the growth of some of the organisms responsible for certain sexually transmitted diseases. However, this hypothesis is still uncertain. The IUD contains a cord that hangs down into the vagina and may inadvertently serve as a sort of passageway into the uterus for infectious germs.

Individuals who make the decision to be sexually active bear the responsiblility to maintain good sexual health for themselves as well as for their partners. Prevention plays an important role in staying well. There are a number of precautions which any sexually active individual may take to minimize his or her chances of contracting or spreading a sexually transmitted disease.

Included among these are learning to recognize any overt signs of sexual diseases and making certain not to engage in sexual activities with a partner who exhibits such symptoms. A cold, clinical examination of one's partner's genitals usually is not feasible, but it is important to try to be alert to revealing symptoms during foreplay. An individual who sees or feels any suspicious sores, blisters, or bumps should immediately ask his or her partner about whatever it is that is of concern. No one should hesitate out of fear of offending his or her partner, since such concern simply reflects a responsible attitude.

If the partner is unable to immediately offer a believable explanation, it is important not to proceed with sexual relations, as an uninfected person may be jeopardizing his or her own good health. This book contains a description of symptoms for each sexually transmitted disease. These sections should be read carefully, since such information will better enable the reader to make accurate and sensible judgements.

The most common sign of sexual disease in both men and women is a discharge. During sexual foreplay the male normally secretes a small amount of clear, odorless fluid from the urethral opening. This natural lubrication is indicative of sexual excitement. However, if a male secretes fluid prior to ejaculation which is foul smelling or cloudy, or if there is any discharge before erection, it may be best to reconsider the originally planned course of action.

In the female, a light, white-colored discharge may be the result of the vagina cleansing itself. In addition, during times of sexual arousal there may be a good deal of slippery, generally odorless lubrication secreted. However, any thick or foul-smelling discharge may be considered suspect.

In some situations, a strong odor can also serve as another telltale sign of sexual infection. Contrary to popular myth, a woman who practices good hygiene need not emit an offensive odor from her genitals. Similarly, the semen ejaculated by a healthy male should not have a harsh, uncharacteristically overpowering odor. However, if either partner emits a strong offensive odor, this may be indicative of a sexual disease, inadequate personal cleanliness, or both.

If the individual's sexual partner claims to be in good sexual health and appears to have no visible symptoms indicative of infection, there are still a number of additional precautions which may be taken to help avoid contracting a sexually transmitted disease. Always urinate following sexual intercourse, as this serves to cleanse the urethra, flushing out some organisms that might eventually cause a urinary tract infection. Wash thoroughly with soap and water both before and after having sexual intercourse. This is especially important for individuals who practice anal intercourse in addition to genital intercourse, since germs are easily transmitted from one area of the body to another.

It is important to thoroughly wash one's hands as well as one's genitals, since bacteria are often inadvertently transmitted during sexual foreplay. The use of a condom is another important protective measure against contracting sexually transmitted diseases. A condom provides a protective barrier which does not allow the disease organisms to spread to another person. Diaphragms and contraceptive foams, jellies, or sponges also may offer some protection. Anyone who has certain knowledge that his or her partner is suffering from a sexually transmitted disease or is currently in the process of being treated for one, should not engage in sexual relations with that individual under any circumstances.

Certain sexual lifestyles increase the risk of contracting a sexually transmitted disease. Individuals who engage in sexual intercourse with multiple partners or prostitutes are at a higher risk. The risk is very low in committed relationships with single partners.

Any sexually active individual should have regular medical checkups which include testing for sexually transmitted diseases to be certain that he or she remains disease free and in good sexual health. However, pelvic examinations are not always routinely done except by gynecologists. Unfortunately, there is still a stigma in our society attached to having a disease that was sexually transmitted. Often people feel guilty, ashamed, and embarrassed when they discover that something of this nature is affecting their lives. In reality, sexually transmitted diseases are not relegated to "bad" or "dirty" people—any sexually active person is at some risk. The organisms do not discriminate and affect people of all ages, races, and socioeconomic backgrounds.

In some instances, long-time family physicians may feel embarrassed by a patient's medical problem brought about through a sexual encounter. They may feel that they may be insulting their patient if they suggest that he or she be routinely tested for sexually transmitted diseases. If the doctor does not work in a clinic specifically designed to treat such diseases, or in a large urban clinic where the diagnosis and treatment of these disorders are routine, he or she may be reluctant to believe that such a "nice young person" has contracted a disease of this type. Many people find this to be especially true of family physicians in small towns who have treated everyone in their family ever since they can remember.

Nonetheless, any person who is sexually active should have a blood test for syphilis (see page 33) as well as yearly tests for gonorrhea (see page 20) and chlamydia (see page 25). Women should also have regular Pap tests and be checked for vaginal infections.

It is every sexually active individual's responsibility to request this type of testing. It is also important that each individual feel sufficiently comfortable with his or her physician to be able to be completely candid regarding the level of his or her sexual activity as well as the specific nature of the sexual practices involved.

Anyone who believes that he or she may have a sexually transmitted disease, or who has recently become sexually active and wishes to initiate routine checkups and testing, may take advantage of several available resources. An individual who has a good relationship with his or her family doctor and believes that physician to be capable of providing objective supportive care while guarding the patient's confidentiality may find this doctor a good source to seek treatment from.

Often individuals feel more comfortable having a sexually transmitted disease treated within a clinic setting. In many instances, the staff is thoroughly familiar with this type of problem, and there may be excellent diagnostic equipment on the premises as well. Most public health departments run free or low-cost STD clinics that provide symptom information and treatment. They can also refer individuals to other clinics which may specialize in particular sexually transmitted diseases. Many communities have other free clinics set up expressly for this purpose. These centers are usually listed in the telephone book, but anyone who experiences difficulty finding the correct number should ask the operator for directory assistance.

Other resources include the Planned Parenthood clinics and affiliates located in forty-two states. In many areas these clinics provide contraceptive information as well as treatment for sexually transmitted diseases. Usually their staff members are supportive to the patient and nonjudgmental in attitude. There is also a VD (venereal disease) National Hotline where trained volunteers provide information regarding sexually transmitted diseases as well as refer individuals to treatment centers in their areas. The toll-free number is 1-800-227-8922. In California call 1-800-982-5882.

In most states, a minor does not need parental approval to be treated for a sexually transmitted disease, and a teenager's confidentiality may be legally guarded. However, a minor who believes that he or she may have contracted a sexually transmitted disease and feels that it is essential that his or her parents or guardians not be informed, should call the treatment center to which he or she intends to go and inquire as to what their policy is regarding the confidentiality of minors. It is not mandatory for a person to furnish his or her parents' or guardians' address in order to be treated for a sexually transmitted disease.

The law requires that a doctor who treats a patient for syphilis, gonorrhea, or AIDS report his or her name to the state health department. This is to enable a public health investigator to contact that person to ensure that all of the individual's sexual contacts are notified of the possibility that they may be infected. Also, in some states doctors must report cases of chlamydia.

Usually these investigators are quite discreet and if, for example, they are contacting a minor at home, they may call, stating to whomever answers the phone something like—they are calling for the school nurse to notify that person that he or she should make an appointment to have a routine hearing test done at school. However, practices vary in different areas and a concerned individual has the right to inquire how his or her partner(s) will be notified. Currently, gonorrhea, syphilis, and AIDS are the only major sexually transmitted diseases which must be reported by law. However, since such diseases may often be fatal or result in serious complications if left untreated, it is essential that every infected person receive treatment under any circumstances, and that all parties involved be contacted.

After reading this book, anyone who suspects that he or she has contracted a sexually transmitted disease should seek treatment immediately. Anyone who has such symptoms as an unusual or increased discharge from the vagina or penis, genital sores, pain during urination, intense itching in the genital area, or abdominal pain should see a physician for an examination.

Many sexually transmitted diseases are most easily diagnosed and treated early. Even if the initial symptoms disappear, the disease remains. Someone who has not been treated has not necessarily been cured. The early symptoms have simply vanished, but the disease may be progressing inside the person's body to a more serious destructive stage. Complications which may result from untreated sexually transmitted diseases are infertility, ectopic pregnancy, and infections and mental retardation of newborns. Some sexually transmitted diseases even result in death.

Most sexually transmitted diseases can be easily treated and cured. Following preventive measures, having regular checkups, and learning to recognize the symptoms or warning signs described in this book are the responsibility of every sexually active individual. Each individual must become the primary guardian of his or her own good health.

* * *

This book describes the various diseases that are spread by sexual activity. The first part of the book covers diseases that are caused by a single organism. The second section describes conditions or syndromes that may be caused by more than one organism. Diagrams of the male and female reproductive systems are included in the final portion of the book, along with a useful glossary.

Symptoms, diagnosis, and treatment are given for each disease. Symptoms are the outward signs of the disease. Diagnosis is the act of identifying the disease. Treatment is the means to get rid of the disease.

PART ONE:

Diseases Caused By a Single Organism

GONORRHEA
CHLAMYDIAL INFECTIONS
LYMPHOGRANULOMA VENEREUM
SYPHILIS
HERPES
GENITAL WARTS
ACQUIRED IMMUNE DEFICIENCY SYNDROME
CHANCROID
DONOVANOSIS
MISCELLANEOUS

GONORRHEA
also known as the clap or the dose

Gonorrhea is generally thought to be among the most prevalent sexually transmitted diseases in America. It is carried by the bacteria *Neisseria gonorrhoeae,* also known as the gonococcus. The gonococcus is able to survive only in the moist, warm atmosphere of the human body's mucous membranes. The most common sites are the genital organs, the rectum, the inside of the throat, and sometimes the eye.

Exposure to light, air, detergent, or water is sufficient to destroy the gonococcus, which therefore makes it almost impossible to contract gonorrhea other than through vaginal, anal, or oral-genital sex with an infected partner.

One of the few exceptions is the gonorrheal eye infections which are most commonly contracted congenitally. When the newborn's eyes come in contact with its mother's infected membranes, the gonococci eat away at the eye's lining and can cause blindness if not treated. However, now all hospitals routinely treat the newborn's eyes with silver nitrate drops or erythromycin to avoid this problem. Eye infections can also be contracted if a person touches the infected area and then puts his or her hand to the eye.

Another exception is that an adult infected with gonorrhea may unknowingly pass this disease to a very young child by drying the child with a towel that has been recently soiled with gonococcal discharge. If the adult doesn't realize that some of the discharge may still be on his or her hands as well, the disease may be transmitted through touch. However, sometimes when a child develops gonorrhea, sexual abuse may be suspected.

Gonorrhea is most commonly transmitted when the mucous membranes of two people touch during sexual contact. Ejaculation by the male need not occur in order to infect his partner. The area of a woman's body most commonly affected by gonorrhea is the cervix. Other areas which may become infected are the urinary passage (urethra), the anus, as well as the Skene's ducts (two small openings on either side of the urinary tract which secrete a fluid to help keep the urinary opening moist) and the Bartholin's glands (glands inside the vaginal opening which secrete a fluid to help keep the vagina moist). Gonorrhea in males most commonly occurs in the urethra, the narrow tube within the penis through which both sperm and urine pass.

Due to the proximity of infection-prone areas of the body, especially in women, gonorrhea may also be spread from one region to another through vaginal discharge, sanitary napkins, or menstrual blood. Anal or oral sex may also spread the disease to the rectum or the throat.

As gonorrhea is highly infectious, it is essential to avoid any sexual activity with anyone who either has gonorrhea or suspects that he or she may have contracted gonorrhea. Having sex with anyone who has recently been exposed to an infected partner jeopardizes the uninfected individual's health.

SYMPTOMS

A large number of women who contract gonorrhea experience no symptoms. In others, weeks or even months may pass until signs of the disease appear. However, most women who do develop symptoms will usually do so between three and twelve days after being infected.

The earliest and most common symptom of gonorrhea in a woman is an increased vaginal discharge. A painful burning sensation during urination may also occur. A physician's examination may reveal that the cervix has become red and swollen, and a discharge may be coming from it. If the rectum has been infected, there may be a mucous discharge from the anus. Defecating may be painful and the stools may be bloody. In instances where the Bartholin's glands are infected, there may be tenderness and swelling at the vaginal opening.

The vast majority of men who become infected with gonorrhea show obvious early symptoms. If the infection occurs in the male's urethra, there may be painful urination. There is almost always a discharge. The discharge may be thin and clear, or thick, creamy, and yellowish in color.

If left untreated, these symptoms may disappear within a few weeks. However, although there may no longer be visible signs of the disease, it often remains present within the body.

If gonorrhea is not recognized and treated at its onset in an infected woman, serious complications may result. The disease can spread upward through the vagina, through the cervix and infect the uterus and fallopian tubes. This complication is called pelvic inflammatory disease, or PID (see page 71). PID can be a complication of many sexually transmitted diseases and occurs in approximately 20 percent of women with gonorrhea. The fallopian tubes become inflamed and swollen and may become filled with pus. Some gonococci may even escape from the tubal area, spilling out into the pelvic cavity. This inflammation may cause the infected individual to experience pain, fever, vomiting, as well as changes in her menstrual cycle. The length of time it takes for an untreated gonorrheal infection to spread upward in a woman's body may vary greatly among individuals. However, PID usually occurs within one month of acquiring gonorrhea.

Pelvic inflammatory disease carries serious consequences. The fallopian tubes become infected and may become permanently blocked, resulting in sterility. At times, a surgical removal of the uterus, fallopian tubes, and ovaries may be necessary, and in some cases the disease has proved to be fatal when left untreated.

Untreated gonorrhea in the male may lead to complications which affect the reproductive organs. The testicles may swell, and the infected individual may experience severe pain in his penis as well as develop abscesses within the urethra. Still another potential danger which may result from gonorrhea that has gone untreated is scarring in the urethra. Scarring narrows the urethra, which in turn causes urination to become extremely painful. In some cases, testicular scarring may cause sterility.

Untreated gonorrhea may result in other serious complications which afflict both men and women. If the gonococci should enter the blood stream, blood poisoning (sepsis) may result. Once the germs freely circulate in the blood stream they are at liberty to attack any organ in the body, causing such ailments as gonococcal arthritis, inflammation of the heart lining (endocarditis), or meningitis. However, if the disease is treated promptly with the proper medication, such complications are unlikely.

DIAGNOSIS

A person who suspects that he or she has gonorrhea can have a culture test or a Gram-stain smear performed. In the culture test, a doctor uses a swab to take a sample of the discharge from the infected area and places it in a culture dish. This is a special environment in which any gonococci present can grow. The culture dish is usually sent to a laboratory where it is observed for twenty-four to forty-eight hours. If gonococci do not appear, the test is negative, and it is highly unlikely that the individual being tested has gonorrhea. If the test is positive, that person must be treated for the disease.

In most cases a culture test is a fairly accurate method for diagnosing gonorrhea. The culture test is the main test for gonorrhea. It is always performed on women, and usually on men. It is more accurate than the Gram-stain test.

In performing the culture test, many doctors will not automatically take a specimen from the anus. However, if an individual who practices anal intercourse suspects that he or she may have gonorrhea, a specimen should be taken from the anus and a culture test performed. Individuals who practice oral-genital sex should have a throat culture taken also. It is possible to have gonorrheal infections simultaneously at more than one site on an individual's body.

Another test, called the Gram-stain test, is perhaps most commonly used in testing for the disease in males who exhibit some symptoms. In a Gram-stain test, a sample of the discharge is taken with a swab, smeared on a glass slide, and stained with a special dye. It is then examined for gonococcal bacteria under a microscope. Magnified, the bacteria look like a small pair of attached beads encased within the walls of a cell.

A negative Gram-stain test still cannot positively assure the individual that he or she is safe. There is always the possibility that the gonococci are still incubating inside the person's body and are not yet visible under a microscope. There's also the chance that the specimen taken for the Gram stain happened to be free of the bacteria even though the person still has gonorrhea. Therefore, the culture test is more commonly used in both men and women.

TREATMENT

It is always best to treat gonorrhea as early as possible before the disease has had a chance to spread. In most cases, gonorrhea is treated with an oral antibiotic, usually a form of penicillin combined with another antibiotic called tetracycline. If an individual is allergic to penicillin, he or she may be treated with tetracycline alone. Ceftriaxone and spectinomycin have been found to be particularly effective against strains of gonorrhea that have become resistant to tetracycline and penicillin.

PPNG (penicillinase-producing *N. gonorrhoeae*) is a strain of gonorrhea especially resistant to penicillin. At first it caused some concern and received a great deal of media coverage as it was thought to be incurable. However, it has since been found that PPNG does respond to ceftriaxone or spectinomycin, so there is less cause for alarm. Also, new treatments which may eventually replace penicillin and spectinomycin are still under development.

A follow-up visit to a doctor or clinic after being treated for gonorrhea is important to make certain that the treatment has been effective and the cure is complete. The physician will determine when and if further cultures should be taken, depending on individual circumstances. In the vast majority of cases the medication does work. If the person still has gonorrhea, it is usually because he or she has been reinfected by a sex partner who is still infected.

SEXUALLY
TRANSMITTED
DISEASES

CHLAMYDIAL INFECTIONS

Chlamydial infections are caused by the bacterium *Chlamydia trachomatis*. These formerly scarcely known infections are spreading across the country in epidemic proportions. Chlamydia is believed to surpass gonorrhea, syphilis, and herpes as the most widespread venereal disease in the United States today. At least three million Americans each year become infected.

The infection is spread through sexual intercourse. When tested, it's been frequently found that the sexual partners of individuals infected with the disease suffer from it as well even though they exhibit no symptoms.

If chlamydia is left unchecked there may be serious consequences. In women, chlamydia looms among the major causes of pelvic inflammatory disease, or PID (see page 71). If the fallopian tubes become blocked by scar tissue, infertility or ectopic (tubal) pregnancy may result. Other complications include miscarriage and premature labor.

Chlamydia trachomatis is a leading cause of nongonococcal urethritis (NGU) in men (see page 76). NGU, which is nearly twice as common as gonorrhea in males, is an inflammation of the urethra which can result in sterility if left untreated. The organism can also be responsible for causing such other conditions as proctitis, a rectal inflammation, and Reiter's syndrome, a kind of arthritis.

Chlamydial infections pose risks for pregnant women and newborns as well. An infected mother may give birth to an infant suffering from an eye infection, which may result in blindness. Or the newborn may have a severe case of pneumonia, which may seriously jeopardize the infant's life.

Chlamydia is a highly infectious disease. Unfortunately, many of its victims exhibit no symptoms of the disease. In fact, the name "chlamydia" is derived from the Greek word *chlamys*, which means "to cloak."

For some other STDs caused by *Chlamydia trachomatis*, refer to lymphogranuloma venereum (see page 26), epididymitis (see page 87), and cervicitis (see page 79).

SYMPTOMS

The infection tends to develop slowly, and at first there may be few or very mild symptoms. When symptoms do exhibit themselves in males, there may be a discharge from the penis and, less commonly, pain upon urination. The discharge is usually less thick than that occurring with gonorrhea. Women may experience an itching or burning sensation in the genital area, a vaginal discharge, and dull pelvic pain.

When symptoms are present, they generally tend to appear within twenty-one days after exposure. Newborns may become infected as they pass through the vaginal canal during birth. Chlamydia is the most common STD in newborns.

The infectious organism, *Chlamydia trachomatis*, attacks the cells lining the genital tract where it multiplies. From there it spreads to the deeper tissues, slowly provoking a damaging inflammatory reaction.

DIAGNOSIS

Chlamydia is sometimes difficult to diagnose since many of the symptoms resemble other sexually transmitted diseases, such as gonorrhea, or because of the lack of symptoms. However, it can be positively diagnosed by a specialized culture test. Another recently developed type of test for chlamydia, called Chlamydiazyme, provides results in only four hours. Other noncultural tests are also available.

TREATMENT

Chlamydia is effectively treated with antibiotics. Usually tetracycline is prescribed to be taken orally for a period of several days. On occasion, erythromycin or sulfa drugs may be prescribed. It is important to take the prescribed medication for the full course of treatment. The infected individual's partner(s) treatment period infected individuals should abstain from having sexual intercourse.

LYMPHOGRANULOMA VENEREUM
also known as LGV or lymphopathia

Lymphogranuloma venereum (LGV) is caused by a strain of *Chlamydia trachomatis.* LGV exists throughout the world, but like some other sexually transmitted diseases such as Donovanosis (see page 52) and chancroid (see page 50), it is largely found in tropical areas. Only about six hundred cases are reported annually in the United States.

The disease, which is generally more common in men, may be transmitted through vaginal, anal, or oral intercourse. The most common form of LGV in the United States today is rectal infection in homosexually active men.

SYMPTOMS

The initial symptoms may occur at any time between one week and three months after an individual has been exposed to an infected partner, although in most newly infected individuals the first signs of the disease appear after about a week.

In some people, nongonococcal urethritis may be the first manifestation of LGV. In others, a small sore surfaces on the sex organs. This painless blister may appear on the cervix, vulva, or on the inner vaginal walls in women, while in men it commonly exists on the penis tip or within the urethra. Some individuals will not even notice the sore as it is painless, may appear in an area of the body where it is not readily visible to the naked eye, and tends to heal and vanish rather rapidly.

However, although the sore may have disappeared, it is certain that the infection has not. Within days the disease spreads to the lymph glands, which will then become swollen and inflamed.

The sensitive, badly inflamed glands may merge, creating a hard, painful lump on the body, which is referred to as a bubo. The lymph nodes may be demolished, and the skin covering the bubo may turn a red-purplish color.

The bubo, which usually appears between one week and one month following the initial sore, will often rupture, draining off a good deal of pus. At the stage at which the bubo is present, afflicted individuals may also experience a loss of appetite, fever, chills, and pain in the joint areas.

If LGV is left untreated, a number of complications may arise. The swollen enlarged lymph vessels in the genital organs of both men and women may block the normal lymph flow, causing an extremely large swelling. This condition is known as elephantiasis and is often accompanied by severe pain.

In addition, if left unchecked LGV may cause pain in the area of the rectum as well as a bloody anal discharge. However, many of these cases are the result of primary rectal infection and not a complication of genital infection. In some cases scar tissue formed in the rectum as a result of the disease may block normal defecation, causing difficult and painful bowel movements. In certain instances, surgery may be required to correct the situation.

It is difficult to determine when and if such complications may arise. The complications described here may arise as late as fifteen years after initially contracting the disease.

DIAGNOSIS

The diagnosis of lymphogranuloma venereum may be tricky as some of its characteristic symptoms resemble those of other sexually transmitted diseases as well as the symptoms of some other diseases which are not transmitted in this manner. However, specific cultures and blood tests have now been developed to test for and positively identify LGV.

TREATMENT

LGV is most often treated with tetracycline taken orally for three to four weeks.

LGV is often regarded as a stubborn disease to get rid of, as it may respond slowly to medication. Infected individuals should check back with their physicians periodically after being treated in order to be certain that their cure is complete.

SEXUALLY
TRANSMITTED
DISEASES

SYPHILIS
also known as lues or bad blood

Syphilis, which is caused by bacteria known as *Treponema pallidum*, is most often transmitted through sexual contact. The syphilis bacteria tend to die quickly when not retained within a warm, moist environment, and therefore it is highly unlikely for an individual to contract syphilis from a toilet seat or towel. However, it is possible to get syphilis through kissing if the infected person has a syphilitic sore in his or her mouth which touches a sore or mucous membrane in his or her partner's mouth. Syphilis may be spread through oral sex and anal sex as well as genital sex.

SYMPTOMS

The earliest symptoms of syphilis generally occur two to six weeks after exposure. However, the initial symptoms may appear at any time ten to ninety days after contact. Unfortunately, many infected women notice no symptoms at all.

The first stage of syphilis is known as the primary stage. The primary stage is characterized by a small, open sore known as a chancre. The chancre is situated at the precise site where the syphilis bacteria originally entered the body. The chancre usually is not very painful and may not be noticed, especially if it is inside the body. The chancre usually goes away in two to four weeks. However, the syphilis infection is still spreading in the body.

The secondary stage of syphilis may erupt anywhere between six weeks and six months after an individual has contracted the disease. The symptoms tend to vary somewhat among different people. However, most individuals experience a skin rash characterized by mildly raised blotches of a pinkish-red color. Usually the rash is painless. It may occur in a symmetrical pattern on dry areas of the body, such as the palms of the hands or the soles of the feet, or anywhere else on the body. If the rash should appear on the scalp, patches of hair may fall out.

When the rash appears on moist areas of the body, it may be seen as slightly raised round or oval open sores which may secrete a clear liquid. Such sores are highly contagious because the fluid oozing from them contains syphilis bacteria in large numbers.

During the secondary stage, the lymph glands may swell and become tender to the touch. Areas most commonly affected are the groin, armpit, and neck. Syphilis sufferers going through the secondary stage sometimes experience an overall feeling of poor health. Fever, headache, a sore throat, loss of appetite, and an overall achy feeling occasionally occur during the second stage.

If the symptoms of the secondary stage are left untreated, they may persist for one to six months. However, it is not uncommon for these symptoms to recur within the next year or two. If an individual learns that he or she has syphilis during the secondary stage, that person should notify all sexual contacts as far back as six months.

It is difficult to predict how any one individual will respond to the secondary stage of syphilis. Some people may experience all of the symptoms described here, while others may suffer from one or two. Still others may experience no symptoms whatsoever. In addition, the severity of secondary stage symptoms may vary greatly among individuals.

If the disease is left untreated during the secondary stage, syphilis will progress to its next phase, which is known as the latent stage. The latent stage is characterized by what appears to be the disappearance of any sign of the disease, although the infected person definitely still has syphilis. The rash vanishes permanently, and the infected person looks and feels as if he or she is enjoying good health.

After about a year following the initial remission of symptoms, the person is no longer contagious and will not pass the disease to others. However, if a blood test for syphilis is administered during this stage, it will read "positive," indicating that the person is still infected with the disease. An individual in the latent stage who first finds that he or she has contracted syphilis should notify all persons with whom he or she has had sexual contact during at least the past year.

It is impossible to know exactly how long any individual infected with syphilis will remain in the latent stage. It may last for just a few years or even a lifetime. During this stage no active damage occurs to the infected person. No one is certain what causes the disease to reactivate itself in some individuals, but approximately one fourth of those with untreated syphilis will advance into the tertiary, or late, stage of syphilis.

The late stage of syphilis may be devastating. The untreated syphilis may attack the eyes, lungs, muscles, brain, nervous system, digestive system, liver, walls of the blood vessels, as well as other organs and areas of the body.

A gumma, an internal or external syphilitic sore which develops during this stage, attacks the body organs and erodes them. If treated, the disease may be stopped at this point, but the damage already inflicted on the infected person's body is irreversible.

At this point syphilis may attack the heart with fatal consequences. It may also destroy certain nerves and may affect the brain and spinal cord so that walking becomes difficult. Syphilis may also be responsible for a condition known as general paresis. Paresis, which involves the brain, can lead to insanity or even death. Individuals afflicted with paresis experience a series of often very unpleasant hallucinations which progress until they are entirely cut off from reality. Such individuals become the victims of their disease-induced terrifying fantasies. Today, however, these conditions are all very rare.

PREGNANCY

It is extremely important to know if a pregnant woman has contracted syphilis, as she may be capable of giving the disease to her unborn child. Syphilis may be passed from a mother to her fetus regardless of what stage of the disease she is in. A baby born with the disease suffers from what is known as congenital syphilis.

If the disease is diagnosed and treated prior to the fourth month of pregnancy, the baby won't develop any symptoms. The fetus is cured simultaneously with its mother's treatment. However, if syphilis is left untreated, a miscarriage or stillbirth may result, or the baby may be born already infected.The child may not experience the characteristic primary or secondary stages of the disease but rather may be born with latent syphilis.

The disease may remain dormant for a number of years before it advances to the next stage (late stage) and furiously attacks the young child's body. However, two thirds of the infected infants have symptoms between the third and eighth week of life; the vast majority have symptoms by three months of age. Some may be born with such birth defects as deafness, blindness, distorted bone structure, and mental retardation. Other serious medical problems may develop soon after birth. Due to these extreme consequences it is advisable for all pregnant women to be tested for syphilis once they learn that they are going to have a child.

DIAGNOSIS

Any sexually active person who develops a sore on the genitals or a suspicious rash anywhere on the body should be tested for syphilis. The doctor will take a scraping from the chancre, if one is present. If an individual practices anal and/or oral sex and has sores in these areas, scrapings from these chancres should be taken as well. The scrapings are then examined under a microscope for the presence of the syphilis bacteria. However, most syphilis cases are diagnosed by a blood test.

If syphilis bacteria are present when the specimen is examined, they will appear as small, moving spirals. A person who is going to have this test performed should make certain not to put any cream or medication of any kind on the sore prior to seeing the doctor. A medicated cream may destroy the germs on the sore's surface and thereby falsify the test results.

Any person who suspects that he or she may have contracted syphilis should also have a blood test to see if the disease is present. A test to diagnose syphilis is used to determine if the individual's blood already contains antibodies to fight off the disease.

TREATMENT

Penicillin is generally used to treat syphilis. Individuals who are allergic to penicillin are often treated with tetracycline or erythromycin taken orally.

Pregnant women who are unable to take tetracycline are treated with erythromycin stearate. This drug is taken by mouth over a period of several weeks.

A reaction with symptoms of fever, headache, nausea, and chills may occur within hours after treatment has begun but usually disappears the following day.

The treatment of syphilis requires follow-up care and testing to make certain that the disease is completely gone.

SEXUALLY
TRANSMITTED
DISEASES

HERPES

The venereal virus herpes simplex is a widespread disease although it is not considered as serious as some other sexually transmitted diseases, such as gonorrhea or chlamydia.

There are many different types of herpes viruses which affect both animals and people, making the herpes virus family an extensive and complex one. However, when people speak about herpes, they are usually referring to herpes simplex type I (oral), and herpes simplex type II (genital).

At one time, herpes simplex type I was thought to only occur in the mouth and facial area. Herpes simplex type II most often appeared below the waist on the genitals, buttocks, and thighs. However, today these distinctions no longer hold true. Individuals who engage in genital sex as well as oral and/or anal sex are susceptible to contracting both forms of the virus in either area of their body. It is also possible for one person to contract both forms of the virus.

Herpes has sometimes been referred to as the "love virus" because it is usually transferred from one person to another through intimate contact. The infection may be spread through kissing or petting as well as through sexual intercourse.

During the first infection of herpes, the virus travels to certain tissues in the body where it remains in a dormant state. Oral herpes migrates from the skin or mouth via the nerves to rest in the ganglia, or deep nerve centers, situated near the brain. Genital herpes rests in the ganglia at the base of the spinal cord.

Usually when the body is infected by a virus, it produces antibodies and special white blood cells to kill the invading germs. These antibodies and white blood cells remain in the individual's system for years, sometimes even for the duration of the person's life, protecting that individual from reinfection by these germs. Like many other viruses and bacteria, herpes viruses stimulate the body to manufacture antibodies and special white cells against them. However, the herpes viruses travel within the body by passing through cell walls that touch one another, and in this way they remain unexposed to surrounding tissue fluids that might contain antibodies and killer white cells.

Factors which may cause a dormant herpes virus to become active and generate another outbreak are generally regarded as varying forms of stress to the body. Among the conditions frequently believed to be responsible for initiating new attacks are a high fever, severe sunburn, pregnancy, and irritation to the genital area.

SYMPTOMS

Although the signs of a first herpes infection may occur between two and twenty-one days after initial exposure to the virus, in the majority of cases an outbreak will appear two to seven days after significant exposure.

Within a short period of time, fluid-filled blisters will usually develop. In women, herpes simplex type II (genital) lesions are spread over the external genitalia as well as inside the vagina.

Females infected with herpes may experience pain when urinating. First infections tend to be extremely painful.

Males who have contracted genital herpes may experience small groups of blisters on or near the penis during an outbreak of the virus. In very severe cases, the penis may swell painfully and the urinary opening may narrow, producing pain and some difficulty in urinating.

The initial outbreak of genital herpes in infected individuals of both sexes may be accompanied by high fever, severe head-ache, and muscle aches and tenderness. Lymph nodes in the groin usually swell during initial episodes. All of these symptoms however, are uncommon in recurrent outbreaks.

One or two days after the blisters appear in an outbreak of genital herpes, the lesions will burst, revealing a raw, reddish area over which a crust or scab may form. This crust will dry up as the lesions heal. Such herpes lesions do not scar the skin.

Genital herpes is highly contagious during the period when the blisters appear. It is less likely to be transmitted once the lesions have formed scabs. However, the danger of contracting genital herpes through sexual intimacies for someone who has never been exposed to the virus is extremely high at any time during his or her partner's outbreak. The virus may even be un-wittingly transmitted during the "warning period," which usually occurs a day or two prior to the outbreak of the blisters. During this period, which is known as the prodrome, the infected individual may experience nothing more than a mild tingling, itching, or burning sensation. However, that person may still be contagious and may be capable of infecting others at this time, although no visible signs of the virus have yet appeared. The prodrome may also occur before the initial herpes attack although it may not be recognized as a warning.

The nature of recurring attacks of the virus may vary greatly among infected individuals. Some fortunate people have had one episode of genital herpes and have never suffered subsequent outbreaks. However, most individuals who have contracted herpes have reported repeated attacks periodically which usually continue for several years. Increasing evidence appears to indicate that the attacks diminish with the passage of time. Longer time spans may occur between outbreaks, and the attacks may appear less severe as well. The blisters that result from recurrent attacks are fewer and often painless. They may be barely noticeable to the casual eye; however, these lesions are highly contagious nonetheless.

Perhaps the greatest danger of contracting genital herpes comes from engaging in sexual activity with a partner who is a "silent carrier." There are some people who contract herpes but never show any visible signs of the virus. Unless for some unusual reason a physician happens to take a virus culture from them during one of their "invisible" outbreaks, they may never even know that they have herpes at all. Unfortunately, they are still quite capable of transmitting the virus to others, and in all likelihood their partners will not become silent carriers as well, but will actively suffer from the symptoms of the virus. Women may develop mild blisters on their cervix or deep inside their vaginal canal where they can't be seen, while some men who have contracted genital herpes never notice a sore on the penis; it is possible that the virus is carried in their semen.

Rectal herpes is usually the result of the herpes virus being transmitted through anal intercourse. This can occur in cases of both heterosexual as well as homosexual relationships. Although the vast majority of rectal herpes cases are contracted through anal intercourse, genital herpes may be spread to the rectal area from the genitals of infected individuals.

Rectal herpes may be extremely painful, as the mucous membrane surrounding the anal opening and inside the rectum may become severely ulcerated. Other symptoms may include itching, chills or fever, and swollen glands in the groin.

Genital herpes may also be spread to other areas of the body through sexual foreplay or masturbation during an obvious outbreak, or by a silent carrier during the period of his or her "invisible" attack. Genital herpes has been spread in this manner to such regions as the lower abdomen, fingers, knees, buttocks, and mouth.

DIAGNOSIS

The diagnosis of genital herpes by a physical examination may be quite accurate if the individual who suspects that he or she has contracted the herpes virus consults the doctor during the time when the lesions or blisters are visible. The doctor may gently wipe a blister with a cotton-tipped swab to take a virus culture or for other tests (for example, a Pap smear, Tzanck preparation, or fluorescent antibody test). Sometimes these tests can detect virus-infected cells more rapidly than the viral culture.

Although there are treatments available that may lessen the symptoms and can sometimes shorten the duration of an attack of herpes simplex type I or type II, medical science has not yet found a cure which will permanently rid the body of the virus. Once herpes has been contracted, the infected individual can expect periodic outbreaks of the virus at various times for an indefinite period.

A drug called acyclovir has proven to be highly effective for initial attacks of herpes. When used to treat patients undergoing a first attack of genital herpes, the drug was shown to shorten the period of pain, itching, and shedding of infectious virus. Acyclovir is often helpful in speeding healing of recurrent attacks. For persons with very severe or frequent episodes, acyclovir can be taken continuously to prevent attacks.

PREVENTION

It is important to try to prevent the infected individual's sexual partner(s) from contracting the disease. Individuals who are free of the virus should learn how to best protect themselves from contracting it as well.

A male who knows or even suspects that he has genital herpes should use a condom when having sex with someone who is free of the virus. A condom can cut down on the incidences of spreading herpes. However, there is no completely effective method to avoid contracting the virus if someone is having repeated sexual contacts with an infected partner.

An individual with obvious herpes blisters on his or her genitals should never have sex with an uninfected partner. Infectious herpes virus may be present in recurring attacks from the first warning symptoms through the full duration of the lesions and scabs.

There are also laboratory studies underway to develop vaccines against herpes viruses.

PREGNANCY

Many young women who fear contracting genital herpes are concerned about the effect the virus may have on future pregnancies. If a woman contracts herpes for the first time while she is pregnant, it is generally believed that her infection will be more severe than if she simply suffers a recurrent herpes attack. Also, primary genital herpes during pregnancy appears to infect infants more often than recurrent attacks. While unproven, it is suspected that contracting herpes during the first few months of pregnancy may cause a miscarriage or growth retardation in the infant.

A woman who contracts herpes either before or during her pregnancy should be closely watched by her obstetrician and monitored by periodic Pap smears and viral cultures. It is crucial that a viral culture be done to test for either active or silent herpes virus which may be present in the birth canal at the approximate time the baby is to be delivered. This culture will help the doctor decide if it is safer for the baby to be delivered through the vagina or by a cesarean section (the baby is removed surgically through the abdomen).

If there's no indication of the virus close to the time of birth, danger to the newborn may be quite minimal. Unfortunately, there is no foolproof guarantee that the baby will not contract herpes even if a cesarean section is performed. In some extremely rare cases, the virus travels through the placenta to the fetus prior to the start of labor.

A pregnant woman with herpes should see her doctor at regular intervals throughout her entire pregnancy. She should also make certain that her doctor is fully informed of her medical history regarding any genital infections as well as if her partner(s) has had an infection of this nature. This information will help the doctor make essential judgements regarding how the pregnancy and delivery will be managed in order to best safeguard the unborn child's welfare.

SEXUALLY
TRANSMITTED
DISEASES

GENITAL WARTS
also known as condylomata acuminata or venereal warts

Genital warts are warts which grow in the region of the genitals and are caused by the human papillomavirus (HPV). Other strains of the same virus also produce warts in other areas of the body. Genital warts may be one of the most common sexually transmitted diseases. Recent findings indicate that HPV may be strongly linked to cancer, particularly cervical cancer.

Genital warts are most commonly transmitted through sexual contact. It has been estimated that more than 65 percent of the persons who engage in sexual contact with a partner who has genital warts will develop warts as well. Pregnancy stimulates the growth of genital warts.

SYMPTOMS

Genital warts, which grow singly or in small groupings, may surface at any time between one and four months after an individual has had sexual contact with an already infected partner. In women they often grow near the vaginal opening, on the outer lips of the vagina, or close to the anus. Genital warts on a man will tend to grow on the tip or shaft of the penis or on the scrotum. Anal warts may be found in homo sexually active men. The warts can cause incessant itching.

A genital wart growing in an area such as the shaft of the penis, which is dry and moisture free, will look very much like the common type of wart we are used to seeing anywhere on the body. However, a genital wart growing in a moist region of the genital area may appear as a small, dark pink bump. These warts tend to grow together, giving the appearance of small clusters of bumps.

Many people infected with HPV—perhaps a majority—do not develop visible warts. But they still carry the virus and can transmit it to a sex partner. Genital warts may affect a Pap smear in women, producing an abnormal reading. Women may also be at risk for complications (for example, cervical cancer) even if visible warts never appear.

DIAGNOSIS

Most doctors can diagnose genital warts by simply examining their appearance. However, special tests (such as a Pap smear) are necessary to detect asymptomatic cases. Everyone with genital warts should be treated as soon as possible. If left untreated, these warts increase in size and number, and may be transmitted to others.

TREATMENT

The treatment determined by the physician will be based on the size and number of the warts as well as on where they are located within the genital area. Most cases of genital warts, however, are treated by freezing with liquid nitrogen. Also, removal by laser surgery is commonly used. Although less effective, podophyllin (a caustic agent) may also be prescribed. Pregnant women cannot use podophyllin as it is known to induce premature labor and can even cause miscarriage as well as fetal congenital abnormalities.

If the treatment is successful, the warts will fall off within several days. In most cases, more than one treatment may be necessary to make certain that all the warts are gone. If even a few warts are left, they may once again grow and multiply. It is especially important for women to have an annual Pap smear even after successful treatment.

Over-the-counter medications should not be used.

ACQUIRED IMMUNE DEFICIENCY SYNDROME
also known as AIDS

Acquired Immune Deficiency Syndrome (AIDS) is a highly publicized disease which has surfaced significantly during the past several years. The National Cancer Institute identified the cause of AIDS as a virus called human lymphotropic virus-III (HTLV-III). Similar findings were reported by the Pasteur Institute in Paris, where the virus was named lymphadenopathy-associated virus (LAV). The virus has also been called AIDS-associated retrovirus (ARV). It is now believed that HTLV-III, LAV, and ARV are the same virus.

The AIDS virus attacks and kills certain white blood cells called T lymphocytes, which help to maintain the body's natural immune system. The immune system protects the body from an extensive variety of diseases. As the virus spreads, the immune system breaks down, leaving the individual susceptible to dangerous infections. The body is no longer capable of effectively eradicating foreign cells that may cause infection or of destroying abnormal cells which may eventually develop into cancer.

AIDS develops slowly over a period of time. It may take six months to five years or more before the symptoms of AIDS appear in an infected individual. So, even if the disease could be permanently halted today, new cases of AIDS would still appear for the next five years.

AIDS exists as a syndrome, which means that a number of different conditions may appear which have all been brought on by the same underlying cause. So far some characteristic patterns have been identified as being associated with AIDS. Stricken individuals are often afflicted with unusual infections called opportunistic infections. Among the most frequently reported is an infection of the lungs called *Pneumocystis carinii* pneumonia (PCP). AIDS victims may also be stricken with otherwise rare forms of cancer, most commonly Kaposi's sarcoma, a form of cancer rarely seen in young people in the United States prior to the AIDS epidemic. The underlying cause for these conditions is a malfunctioning of the immune system, which is the essence of AIDS.

The AIDS virus may also attack the brain cells, causing mental deterioration with or without other symptoms.

The AIDS virus is most commonly transmitted through sexual contact, primarily anal intercourse. The virus has been found in some body fluids, such as semen and blood. Infection has also occurred through the use of contaminated hypodermic needles and through transfusions of contaminated blood. The AIDS virus is not transmitted through coughing, sneezing, or just by touching an infected individual.

While technically anyone is capable of contracting AIDS, some individuals are more likely to become AIDS victims. People who fall into this category are members of certain high-risk groups.

So far about 70 to 75 percent of AIDS victims in the United States have been homosexually active men. About 15 to 20 percent of cases are in the intravenous drug user group.

Cases of AIDS have also been noted among hemophiliacs, who are individuals with an inherited blood clotting problem. These individuals appear to have contracted AIDS through a blood factor which entered their bodies through transfusions of donated blood. It is now certain that AIDS may be transmitted to anyone through blood transfusions.

The infants born to mothers having AIDS comprise still another group in serious jeopardy of contracting the disease.

At this point most of the women who have contracted AIDS were intravenous drug users. Others have been sexual partners of people with the AIDS virus or were prostitutes.

AIDS is generally considered a fatal disease; very few people have lived past three years following their diagnosis of AIDS.

Recent research has revealed that numerous homosexually active men show deficiencies in their immune system to some degree. As of early 1986, federal health officials have speculated that in addition to the already diagnosed persons with AIDS, 500,000 to 1 million or more Americans have been infected by the AIDS virus. Some individuals are symptomless carriers of the virus, while others may exhibit such symptoms as weight loss, fever, swollen lymph nodes, or diarrhea. This syndrome is called AIDS-related complex, or ARC. The majority of persons with this syndrome have not developed any of the life-threatening complications associated with AIDS.

Whether or not these individuals who appear to be suffering from an early or mild form of AIDS will eventually develop the more serious complications associated with the syndrome is still unknown at this time. Some studies suggest that between 5 and

20 percent of these individuals may eventually develop overt AIDS over a period of months to years.

SYMPTOMS

There is no one specific symptom which will clearly identify an individual as having AIDS. The symptoms associated with AIDS relate to the various illnesses that characterize the AIDS syndrome.

The early symptoms of AIDS may often seem similar to experiencing a bad cold or flu. In fact, many of the same signs are also seen in less serious medical disorders. AIDS symptoms tend to develop gradually. Often AIDS victims were aware of these symptoms several months prior to their diagnosis, but had not sought medical attention because they believed that nothing was seriously wrong with them. Any individual who is a member of one of the high-risk groups previously described, experiencing one or more of the following symptoms, does not necessarily have AIDS but should seek medical attention for positive verification.

The signs to be alert for are
- Significant weight loss of over ten pounds that is unrelated to diet or exercise
- Swollen lymph nodes or glands
- Feelings of fatigue and general malaise
- Persistent fevers
- Sweating at night
- Continuous coughing or shortness of breath
- Swelling and tenderness of joints, bruising easily, or unusual and prolonged bleeding
- Headaches, confusion, significant shifts in personality
- Persistent skin irritations or lesions inside the mouth, nose, or anus, or purplish marks or bumps on the skin anywhere on the body

Persistent diarrhea

Thrush, a thick white coating on the tongue or in the throat which persists

TREATMENT

At this time, there is no cure or vaccine for AIDS. Antibiotics and other drugs are currently used to fight each separate infection resulting from AIDS, but eventually the body's immune system completely deteriorates.

Research continues on experimental drugs which either attack the AIDS virus directly or aim at rebuilding the immune system.

One advance that has occurred is a test that identifies antibodies to the AIDS virus in blood supplies.

There is a great deal of research which needs to be done in order to gain more insight into this still baffling illness.

PRECAUTIONS

In order to reduce the possibility of contracting AIDS, the following precautions should be adhered to:

Do not use recreational drugs—it is imperative never to use a drug which is taken intravenously.

Avoid sexual contact with anyone who is an intravenous drug user or who has had a large number of sexual partners.

Sexually active individuals should limit the number of their sexual partners.

Avoid sexual contact with anyone suffering from swollen glands or who has any of the AIDS symptoms previously listed.

Be sure to get plenty of rest, proper nutrition, and adequate exercise.

Use a condom when engaging in intercourse or fellatio.

Maintain good personal hygiene.

SEXUALLY
TRANSMITTED
DISEASES

CHANCROID
also known as "soft chancre"

Although a common disease throughout other regions of the world, chancroid generally exists in tropical climates and is not widespread in the United States. Under 1,000 cases are annually reported in this country.

The disease is caused by a miniscule rod-shaped bacterium known as *Haemophilus ducreyi*. The bacterium, which most often enters the body through a scrape or crack in the skin on the genitals, is usually transmitted through oral, anal, or genital intercourse.

SYMPTOMS

The initial symptoms generally appear between two and seven days after an individual has had sexual contact with an infected partner. In some cases, it may take as long as two weeks for the first symptoms to surface. Some people contract the disease without showing any visible symptoms, although such cases are uncommon.

The earliest symptom is the appearance of one or more small reddish bumps or pimples in the genital area. In women such small blisters generally arise on the cervix, vagina, vulva, or anus; in men the bumps most often appear on the penis shaft, the foreskin, or the anus. The small blisters soon turn into open sores. Unlike the chancre of syphilis, these sores are painful and may bleed when touched. Pus emitted from them may give off a foul-smelling odor. The sores may spread to other regions of the body near or adjacent to the genital area, such as the groin, thighs, and stomach.

In many cases the lymph nodes may become infected. In such instances there may be painful swelling, which usually indicates destruction of the affected tissues by the disease. Further complications may arise as the pus drains from the lymph nodes, making the individual highly susceptible to infection by other bacteria.

DIAGNOSIS

Chancroid may often be suspected upon visual examination by a physician. However, chancroid is sometimes confused with other genital lesions, such as those found in syphilis or herpes. A culture of the chancre should be taken as further confirmation.

TREATMENT

Chancroid may be treated differently by various physicians. Antibiotics are used, especially erythromycin, trimethoprim with suflamethoxazole, or ceftriaxone. Some doctors prescribe sulfa drugs or tetracycline. Chancroid is usually considered to be over once the ulcerous sores have completely healed. However, as reinfection with this disease is common, infected individuals should be certain to secure a follow-up examination after being medicated.

SEXUALLY TRANSMITTED DISEASES

DONOVANOSIS
also known as granuloma inguinale or granuloma venereum

Donovanosis is generally thought of as a sexually transmitted disease, although it has not been positively proven that the disease cannot be transmitted in other ways as well. Donovanosis is caused by a bacterium known as *Calymmatobacterium granulomatis.*

The disease usually occurs only in tropical climates. Less than one hundred cases have been reported in the United States yearly, with the majority of these appearing in the South.

SYMPTOMS
The symptoms of the disease may appear at any time between several days and three months after the initial contact with an infected partner. The disease is spread by coming in direct contact with a Donovanosis lesion. This infection tends to grow slowly and often some time elapses before even the initial symptoms of the disease appear.

The earliest symptoms look like small bumps or pimples. In women they usually erupt on the vulva, cervix, or near the anus, while in men the small bumps often appear on the penis tip, beneath the foreskin, as well as in the area of the anus.

The initial bumps, which are usually painless at first, soon transform into tender reddish sores. The sores may bleed or ooze pus. At times they may become quite painful as well as give off a foul odor. The sores tend to spread. If they should spread to the urinary or rectal openings, urination and defecation may become quite difficult and painful. The painful sores as well as the general tenderness of the immediate area may make intercourse uncomfortable.

DIAGNOSIS

A physician will usually base his or her diagnosis of Donovanosis on the appearance of the symptoms combined with a microscopic examination of the infected tissue to identify the characteristic bacteria formation.

TREATMENT

Donovanosis is usually treated with tetracycline. For individuals unable to take tetracycline, such as pregnant women, another antibiotic, ampicillin, is commonly substituted. Most doctors prescribe the drug to be taken orally four times a day for a period of two to three weeks. The ampicillin is usually taken over a longer period of time with the exact number of weeks being determined by the infected individual's physician. All infected individuals should return to their doctors for follow-up examinations after they have begun their course of treatment. Once the inflammation has disappeared, the lesions have healed, and only the scars remain, the individual is generally regarded as cured.

MISCELLANEOUS

Pubic Lice, Scabies, Molluscum Contagiosum,
Viral Hepatitis, Cytomegalovirus, The Genital
Mycoplasmas, The Enteric Pathogens

PUBIC LICE
also known as crabs or pediculosis pubis

Pubic lice are miniscule, wingless insects of a grayish brown or white color which attach themselves to pubic hairs. They feed on the small blood vessels in the area by attaching their mouths to the hair follicle.

Pubic lice are difficult to see with the naked eye. Often they may appear to be a speck of dirt or a flake of skin, but when removed from the pubic area, movement of the insects' legs may be visible. Although lice generally attach themselves to pubic hair, they can also exist on other hairy parts of the body, such as the underarms, eyebrows, or the hairy areas of the chest.

Pubic lice die within twenty-four hours unless attached to a human host. When attached to a human body, they will survive for approximately thirty days. They mate with tremendous frequency and lay up to three eggs a day. These eggs, known as nits, are oval shaped and of a grayish-white hue. They are usually found attached to the hair shaft close to the skin (near where the hair follicle touches the skin) and will hatch in approximately nine days after they are laid. Once hatched, these new lice will begin to reproduce after seventeen days.

Pubic lice may be easily transmitted from one individual to another. They are most often transmitted during sexual intercourse; however, if a couple were nude, an infested person could easily transmit pubic lice to his or her partner through a close caress. Lice may also be picked up from a towel, bedding, articles of clothing, or even occasionally from a toilet seat which has been infested with lice or their eggs.

SYMPTOMS

Perhaps the most noticeable symptom of pubic lice is mild itching in the pubic area. It is generally thought that the itching is brought on by an allergic skin reaction to the saliva which the lice secrete as they feed. Although most infested individuals develop this reaction, there are many people who do not, so it is not unusual to have lice and be symptomless.

The itching may often cause infested persons to scratch the area, which provides little relief and in fact may intensify the itching sensation. In some people, lice may cause a slight rash of small, bluish dots.

DIAGNOSIS

There are no specialized medical tests to diagnose pubic lice. They may easily be diagnosed visually upon inspection by a physician. However, as an initial infestation may involve less than ten lice, they may be difficult to locate at the start. Often it is easier to see the nits.

TREATMENT

Treatment for lice entails ridding the body as well as any infested clothing, bed linen, towels, and toilet seats of the lice or their eggs. For the body, a doctor may prescribe a lotion, shampoo, or cream which contains gamma benzene hexachloride, such as Kwell. This medication kills the lice and their eggs. However, it has some disadvantages and should not be used on small children, pregnant women, or individuals with lesions on the scrotum.

If the prescribed shampoo or lotion is not used, there are a number of over-the-counter remedies that may be purchased at most drugstores or pharmacies. A pharmacist is qualified to recommend one.

Since lice can survive for a time on towels, clothing, bed linens, as well as on other articles of this sort, such items must be laundered. Once separated from a human host, lice may live for up to twenty-four hours. The separated eggs will hatch within seven to ten days. Any article suspected of being infested should be washed well in hot water or dry cleaned. In addition, the toilet and toilet seat should be thoroughly scrubbed with a strong disinfectant.

* * *

SCABIES

Scabies is a contagious skin infection caused by the parasite *Scarcoptes scabiei*. It is a tiny, white, eight-legged mite which burrows in the skin to deposit eggs. Although scabies is transmitted through sexual contact and has recently become quite common on the external genitals, it may be passed to others through nonsexual contact as well. Scabies is often found in children, usually in the skin around the wrists, between the fingers, and on the elbows.

SYMPTOMS

An individual with scabies may experience severe itching. Small red bumps are present on the skin. The rash is usually prominent and can occur anywhere, but most often on the hands, lower abdomen, and vaginal area.

DIAGNOSIS

An experienced physician often can diagnose scabies by the appearance of the rash. However, to be certain, the mite must be extracted by scraping it from the skin and then examined under a microscope by a physician.

TREATMENT

To rid the body of scabies, a shampoo, lotion, or cream containing gamma benzene hexachloride, such as Kwell, is usually prescribed. It should be noted that itching may persist for one to two weeks after successful treatment.

* * *

MOLLUSCUM CONTAGIOSUM

Molluscum contagiosum is a condition which is characterized by small, smooth, white raised bumps or growths on the genital organs of both males and females. The bumps, which often have a depression in the center, may appear in clusters.

The disease is caused by a virus. It may be transmitted in ways other than through sexual contact, such as through various forms of close contact as well as in swimming pools. In fact, previously most victims of molluscum contagiosum were children who showed evidence of the disease in other areas of their body.

However, in recent years there has been a marked increase of molluscum contagiosum appearing on the genitals of adults, who usually acquire the disease by sexual contact.

SYMPTOMS

Molluscum contagiosum is painless and exhibits no other symptoms. The initial bumps may appear anytime between twenty-one and ninety days after exposure, although there have been instances in which a longer period of time elapsed.

DIAGNOSIS

The disease is recognizable to a physician by the appearance of the small bumps.

TREATMENT

Many doctors prefer not to treat molluscum contagiosum, as the disease sometimes tends to disappear by itself as mysteriously as it appeared. However, it is usually treated in adults to prevent spreading of the disease. Molluscum lesions may be scraped off with a surgical instrument called a curette. In some cases, medication may be applied to prevent recurrences.

* * *

VIRAL HEPATITIS

Hepatitis is an inflammation of the liver. Although the hepatitis viruses may be contracted through a variety of modes, one of the ways they are acquired is by sexual transmission.

There are a number of different viruses that cause the spread of different forms of hepatitis. The various forms of hepatitis may be similar in the symptoms produced, yet they may be transmitted in different manners.

One form of hepatitis is called hepatitis A or infectious hepatitis. The virus is present in the feces of infected persons and can easily be spread through anal-oral sex or other forms of sexual contact which may involve ingesting even a miniscule amount of feces. However, the vast majority of hepatitis A cases are contracted through such nonsexual means as eating food or drinking water which has been contaminated by sewage. It can also be transmitted through food which has been contaminated by an individual infected with the disease.

Another form of hepatitis is called hepatitis B. This form may be transmitted through blood transfusions, contaminated needles, as well as through all the bodily fluids, such as saliva, semen, perspiration, urine, menstrual blood, and vaginal secretions of an infected individual. Thus, hepatitis B may be easily transmitted through sexual intercourse. Although hepatitis B may be contracted by anyone regardless of gender, statistically, men are more likely to be the victims. This appears to be particularly true for homosexually active men. There is a risk of permanent liver damage and liver cancer as late complications of the disease.

There are different forms of hepatitis caused by viruses which are neither A nor B, but at the present time not a great deal is known about these types of viral hepatitis.

SYMPTOMS

The symptoms of hepatitis may vary from mild to severe, depending on the individual case. Some people who suffer from a mild case of hepatitis claim that they feel as though they simply have a bad case of the flu. More severe symptoms may include chills, fever, a general feeling of weakness, nausea, an itching sensation, and a condition known as jaundice, in which the skin and whites of the eyes take on a yellowish hue. If the infected individual should become jaundiced, his or her urine may turn brownish; occasionally the stools may become a light gray color. Severe cases of hepatitis may result in death.

A large percentage of people who contract hepatitis never experience any symptoms. However, these individuals are still capable of transmitting the disease to others through sexual contact and other means.

DIAGNOSIS

If an infected individual experiences jaundice, the yellowish tint of his or her skin will usually lead a physician to suspect that the patient is suffering from hepatitis. However, approximately half of the people who contract hepatitis have mild cases during which jaundice may not set in.

If an individual suspects that he or she has hepatitis or has been exposed to the disease, that person should see a doctor. Through the use of blood tests, the doctor can determine what type of hepatitis the individual is suffering from as well as the extent of liver damage.

TREATMENT

The only cure for hepatitis is plenty of rest and nutritious food. People suffering from hepatitis may feel weak and exhausted much of the time, so although it may not be necessary to remain in bed continuously, it is important for the infected person to rest.

Although one's appetite tends to diminish during a bout of hepatitis, it is important for the infected individual to continue eating, as nutrients for the body are essential at this time. Some people prefer to eat small meals numerous times throughout the day if they don't feel able to tackle three large meals. It is important not to take any type of medication or ingest even small amounts of alcohol until such actions have been approved by a doctor. Liquor may potentially harm the liver, so it might be necessary to wait up to six months or even longer to again drink alcohol, depending on the individual set of circumstances.

PREVENTION

A highly effective vaccine to prevent hepatitis B has been perfected. It is currently used in the United States to immunize hospital workers and other medical personnel who are considered at high risk of contracting the disease. Most importantly, the vaccine is recommended for homosexually active men and for partners of people with chronic hepatitis B. There is also a hepatitis B immune globulin for people who have had recent exposure to someone with hepatitis B.

If an individual knows that he or she has been exposed to hepatitis A, that person may be able to avoid the onset of the disease by seeing a physician and getting an injection of immune serum globulin (ISG) soon after the initial exposure. If the shot of ISG, also known as gamma globulin, does not fully prevent the disease, it may lessen the impact and severity of the symptoms.

Hepatitis is most dangerous for a pregnant woman when it is contracted either very early or very late in her pregnancy. Early on it increases the risk of spontaneous abortion, while much later it may induce early labor. As immune serum globulin may be taken by pregnant women without risk to either themselves or to the fetus, any pregnant woman who has been exposed to hepatitis should seek medical attention immediately.

* * *

CYTOMEGALOVIRUS

Cytomegalovirus (CMV) infection is caused by a member of the herpes virus family. It is an infection which may be transmitted through sexual contact as well as other types of contact. It has been found in the urine, saliva, blood, cervical secretions, semen, and breast milk of infected individuals.

The severity of CMV infection depends a great deal on the age and health of the infected individual. The most severe cases are found in fetuses who become infected through the placenta before birth. Infection may spread to the central nervous system and liver and cause death *in utero*. Infants may also become infected either during delivery by inhaling the infected mother's cervical secretions or shortly after birth from infected breast milk. Infants may be born with mental retardation, motor disabilities, hearing loss, or liver disease. Congenital CMV is the most significant viral cause of mental retardation in infants.

SYMPTOMS

Most adults with CMV infection have no symptoms. However, when symptoms occur, they are similar to those of infectious mononucleosis, with fever and swollen lymph glands. Some individuals with CMV also experience sore throat or liver problems. Severe CMV infections in adults are rare and are usually found in individuals who already have other types of debilitating diseases.

In children, CMV infection is almost always asymptomatic and is usually shed in urine and saliva for several months without harm to the individual.

DIAGNOSIS

CMV infection is diagnosed by identifying the virus from urine, semen, saliva, blood, cervical secretions, breast milk, or tissues of infected individuals. A culture test is usually performed.

TREATMENT

There is no treatment for cytomegalovirus infection. Testing continues on various drugs and vaccines, but most cases of CMV infection are mild and the symptoms go away by themselves.

* * *

THE GENITAL MYCOPLASMAS

The mycoplasmas are organisms which cause a variety of diseases including pelvic inflammatory disease and nongonococcal urethritis. The mycoplasmas which usually cause human genital disease are *Ureaplasma urealyticum* and *Mycoplasma hominis.*

Infection by genital mycoplasmas usually occurs through sexual contact. However, infants may become infected as they pass through the birth canal. Mycoplasmas have been found in the nose and throat of some infants.

In men, genital mycoplasmas infect the urethra. They can also be found under the foreskin of uncircumcised men. In women, the genital mycoplasmas are often found in the vagina.

The symptoms associated with genital mycoplasmas vary depending on the disease caused by the mycoplasma. The presence of genital mycoplasmas can be determined through culture tests.

Treatment for infection with genital mycoplasmas depends upon the syndromes for which the mycoplasmas may be responsible. In cases of pelvic inflammatory disease and nongonococcal urethritis, tetracycline is used. If the disease is resistant to tetracycline, other medications such as erythromycin may be prescribed.

* * *

THE ENTERIC PATHOGENS

The enteric pathogens are bacteria, viruses, and other organisms which cause inflammation of the intestine and rectum. The enteric pathogens are an important cause of diarrheal disease. Enteric pathogens were once associated with contaminated food or water, but now these organisms have been found to be transmitted through sexual contact as well. The most common form of sexual transmission is through oral-anal contact. Homosexually active men are increasingly infected by the enteric pathogens.

Four common enteric pathogens—shigellosis, campylobacter, giardiasis, and amebiasis—are described below.

Shigellosis

Shigellosis is an intestinal infection. Although it is usually not serious, severe cases of shigellosis, also called bacillary dysentery, may be characterized by abdominal cramps, diarrhea with blood and mucus, fever, nausea, and vomiting. However, mild and asymptomatic infections of shigellosis are common. The infection usually lasts an average of four to seven days.

Shigellae, the disease organisms, may be transmitted through sexual contact, especially in homosexual men. Most cases in other persons, however, are acquired through nonsexual means, primarily through contaminated food or water. Shigellosis may also be acquired by infants during birth.

Shigellosis often occurs in two phases. The first phase lasts one to three days, and an individual may experience fever, cramping, abdominal pain, diarrhea, and dehydration. The second phase may last for several weeks. In this phase, fever is usually absent but the number of bowel movements increases and the feces may contain bright red blood and mucus. The individual may lose weight and feel weak in this phase. Straining during defecation and urination is common. Some individuals may experience the first phase but not the second.

In children with shigellosis, high fever and convulsions may be major symptoms. Headache, delirium, drowsiness, and other neurologic symptoms are common in children although they are rare in adults.

Shigellosis is usually suspected in any patient with fever and diarrhea. Blood and mucus in the feces may indicate the more severe type of shigellosis, bacillary dysentery. The diagnosis should be confirmed through culture tests which isolate the disease organisms.

Shigellosis is treated with antibiotics such as ampicillin or the combination of sulfamethoxazole and trimethoprim. Although the disease organism is usually excreted from the body within two weeks, antibiotics decrease the duration of diarrhea and other symptoms. Antidiarrheal medications should not be used. An individual with shigellosis should drink plenty of fluids to prevent dehydration. Sheets and bedclothes which may be infected should be cleaned or discarded.

Individuals with shigellosis should avoid sexual contact until the infection is gone. Sexual partners should also be examined.

Campylobacter

Campylobacter infections are a common cause of diarrheal and intestinal disease. The bacterium which causes intestinal infection in humans is called *Campylobacter fetus* subspecies *jejuni.*

Campylobacter infections are often spread through sexual contact which involves intake of fecal matter, but they are most commonly acquired through contact with infected animals, eating inadequately cooked poultry or beef, or drinking unpasteurized milk or contaminated water.

The most common symptom of campylobacter is diarrhea, which may be preceded by one to two days of fever, nausea, headache, backache, vomiting, or abdominal pain. Bloody diarrhea or diarrhea with mucus may be seen in some cases. Without treatment, symptoms usually last about seven days. Some individuals with campylobacter infections have no symptoms.

Campylobacter fetus subspecies *jejuni* can be detected through culture tests.

Campylobacter infections are treated with appropriate antibiotics such as erythromycin or tetracycline. Since asymptomatic infections are common, sexual partners of individuals with campylobacter should be examined to prevent spread of the disease.

Giardiasis

Giardiasis is a protozoan infection caused by the organism *Giardia lamblia.* Giardiasis usually occurs in the small intestine and is often asymptomatic. However, it may also be associated with symptoms such as diarrhea, abdominal pain, bloating, fatigue, weight loss, and nausea.

Among homosexual men, giardiasis is usually sexually transmitted through oral-anal contact. Children and heterosexual adults usually become infected through ingesting contaminated food and water.

When symptoms are present, the most common one is diarrhea which may last ten days or more. Sometimes the diarrhea is accompanied by nausea, vomiting, and fever. Giardiasis may last six to seven weeks.

Diagnosis of giardiasis is made through examination of feces for the disease organism. Usually, it is necessary to examine more than one fecal specimen.

Giardiasis is treated with antigiardial medications such as quinacrine hydrochloride or metronidazole.

Amebiasis

Amebiasis is an infection caused by a species of intestinal ameba called *Entamoeba histolytica*. The infection usually occurs in the intestine, but it may spread to the liver and lungs.

E. histolytica may be transmitted through sexual contact in which fecal matter may be ingested and is a common STD in homosexual men. As in the case of other intestinal infections, however, most infections in heterosexual adults and children are acquired by nonsexual means, especially contaminated water.

In areas where nutritional and hygienic conditions are good, amebiasis may occur without symptoms. However, in areas where sanitation and nutrition are poor, amebiasis may cause serious disease and death if untreated. Symptoms include diarrhea which may be bloody or streaked with mucus. Fever, chills, cramping, and abdominal pain may be present. The diarrhea may be alternated with periods of constipation and may last for one to four weeks. In severe cases of amebiasis, diarrhea may occur up to eighteen times a day and may be accompanied by weight loss and anemia.

Amebiasis should be suspected in cases of severe diarrhea, especially when the feces contain blood or mucus. However, the diagnosis of amebiasis depends on the microscopic identification and/or isolation of *E. histolytica* from the feces. Some anti-diarrheal medications and other substances interfere with detection of *E. histolytica*. Thus, a history of medications should be obtained for individuals being tested for amebiasis.

Symptomatic infections of amebiasis should be treated with metronidazole. Asymptomatic infections should be treated with diiodohydroxyquin or metronidazole. Once treatment is finished, fecal specimens should be examined in one-month intervals for three months to be certain the disease is gone.

PART TWO:
Diseases Caused By More Than One Organism

PELVIC INFLAMMATORY DISEASE
NONGONOCOCCAL URETHRITIS
CERVICITIS
VAGINAL INFECTIONS
EPIDIDYMITIS

PELVIC INFLAMMATORY DISEASE
also known as PID or salpingitis

Pelvic inflammatory disease (PID) is the general term used to describe inflammations of the organs in the pelvic region. It is a disease which affects only women. PID is the most common complication of STD in women and among the most serious. It is the most common cause of infertility in women.

Numerous organisms may be responsible for causing PID, some of which may be originally transmitted to the vagina through sexual intercourse. PID is almost always directly caused by other sexually transmitted diseases, most commonly chlamydia and gonorrhea. The organisms which cause these other sexually transmitted diseases, such as *chlamydia trachomatis* and the gonococcal organism, travel up from the vagina or cervix through the uterus and into the fallopian tubes. The infection may fill the length of the tubes and spill out to infect the ovaries. It may also pour out into the pelvic cavity.

Generally, a woman's cervix serves as a natural barrier to prevent bacteria in the vagina from travelling upward to the pelvic organs. However, with PID, the bacteria manage to enter the cervix. It is still not known how these organisms are transported into the pelvic region, but it may be possible that they are transported by sperm to the uterus and tubes. The gonococci of gonorrhea commonly attach themselves to human sperm.

In addition, the cervical canal is slightly dilated each month during a woman's period to allow the flow of menstrual blood. The bacteria responsible for gonorrhea thrive extremely well on menstrual blood, and the initial symptoms of PID caused by gonorrhea often appear for the first time following a woman's period. Thus, menstrual blood may be another transporter of these organisms. But transportation by menstrual blood and sperm are possible only for gonococcal PID and not other types of PID.

Women who use intrauterine devices (IUDs) as a form of contraceptive run a much greater risk of getting PID than women who do not use them.

When the infection spreads through the fallopian tubes, there may be a great deal of pus created as the body attempts to defend itself against the invading organisms. As bands of scar tissue, called adhesions, form within the tube, the tube may become either partially or completely blocked. These blockages are called tubal occlusions.

If the infection also exists in the pelvic cavity as well as in the tubes, adhesions or pelvic abscesses may form. Any of these abscesses may rupture and damage or destroy the tubes.

Further complications may also arise if extensive adhesions are formed which block the movement of the tubes as well as other organs in the pelvic area. Tubal blockages, abscesses, and extensive adhesions involved in cases of PID may result in infertility or sterility for the infected individual.

SYMPTOMS

PID symptoms may vary, depending on the type of bacteria which is initially responsible for the infection. Other factors which affect the type and severity of PID symptoms are the strength of the particular strain of the infectious bacteria, the particular organs which are affected by the spread of the disease, and the effectiveness of the infected woman's bodily resistance to the disease.

Some of the more common symptoms associated with PID are low abdominal pains, cramps, fever, chills, backaches, vaginal discharge, abnormal menstrual bleeding, frequent urination, cramping of abdominal muscles, and nausea. These symptoms will usually range from mild to severe and may develop gradually or appear all at once without warning. However, some PID—especially that due to chlamydia—may be symptomless, and yet still lead to infertility due to tubal blockage.

DIAGNOSIS

If a woman complains of the symptoms outlined above, her physician may suspect that she has pelvic inflammatory disease.

An internal examination may show pus dripping from the cervix. A physician will usually take a sample of the discharge and perform a culture test. This may help the doctor to isolate exactly which type of germ is responsible for the infection so that he or she can prescribe the most effective medication.

The diagnosis of PID may sometimes be tricky, since the disease may easily be mistaken for a number of different conditions, such as appendicitis, an ovarian cyst rupture, or an ectopic pregnancy (tubal pregnancy).

Mild cases with few symptoms tend to disguise the real risk involved with PID. Even though the woman may not be experiencing severe discomfort at any given moment, the infection still exists in her body and may later cause painful attacks or even more serious consequences.

Doctors may employ ultrasound or X-ray examinations in cases that present special diagnostic difficulties. In some instances, the only way to be assured of a definitive diagnosis is through a laparoscopic examination. In such cases a small surgical incision is made in the abdominal wall through which specialized viewing instruments are inserted.

TREATMENT

Many authorities agree that individuals with pelvic inflammatory disease should be hospitalized and given antibiotics intravenously. However, many doctors treat mild cases of PID with oral antibiotics. Ampicillin and tetracycline are most commonly prescribed.

The disease should be treated as early as possible, for although the spread of the disease may be checked at a later stage, in some cases the damage already caused to the infected individual's body may be beyond repair. It is important to take the entire dose of medication for the full period of time prescribed in order to prevent flare-ups and reduce the chance of infertility.

The infected individual should also try to remain in bed until her fever is gone and the pain has ceased. Moving about may jar the uterus and tubes, further aggravating the inflammation.

Throughout treatment the patient should drink plenty of water to prevent dehydration, especially if fever is present. She should not engage in sexual intercourse while she is recovering. As such sexual contacts may move the pelvic organs, there is always the danger of spreading pus throughout an even larger area.

In some cases, PID may turn into a chronic condition. Stubborn bacteria may become sealed off by adhesions or lie deep within pelvic abscesses where they cannot be fought by the antibiotics given to treat the disease. In these cases, it may be possible to operate and drain the abscesses. If this is not possible and antibiotics taken both orally and intravenously have not been successful, a hysterectomy may be necessary to relieve the infected individual of chronic pain and infection. In some more-severe cases, uterus, tubes, and ovaries may be removed.

However, a woman should first explore all other alternatives with her physician before consenting to such procedures. In some instances, it may be possible to have the uterus surgically removed while allowing at least one ovary to remain to prevent early menopause. This may grant the woman relief from the pain.

All women become susceptible to repeated infection, and at times these smoldering infections may flare up into very painful, acute attacks of PID. Therefore, women should take some preventive measures to try to avoid a recurrent attack. Medical treatment should be obtained for all vaginal infections at the first sign of symptoms. Gonorrhea and chlamydia cultures should be taken routinely if the nature of a woman's sexual contacts warrants them. If a woman has suffered from previous pelvic infections, a birth control method other than the IUD is recommended.

All sexual contacts of an infected individual should also be treated, and follow-up cultures should be taken to prevent repeat infections.

NONGONOCOCCAL URETHRITIS
also known as NGU or nonspecific urethritis (NSU)

Nongonococcal urethritis (NGU) is an inflammation of the urethra, the tube that carries urine from the bladder. It is usually
caused by the bacterium *Chlamydia trachomatis* (see page 23) or
Ureaplasma urealyticum. NGU infects more than three million
Americans each year and is the most common sexually transmitted disease in men. NGU is at least twice as common as gonorrhea in men.

This disease is characterized by a mildly painful burning
sensation upon urination or a discharge from the urethra. NGU
is usually transmitted through sexual intercourse with a partner
who is already infected with the disease-producing organisms.
The disease may also be transmitted to the eyes by hands which
have come in contact with the NGU-producing organisms and
which have not been thoroughly washed.

SYMPTOMS
The symptoms in the male, painful urination and a discharge,
are similar to those of gonorrhea but in general less severe. In
fact, an individual infected with gonorrhea who has been suc-

cessfully treated for the disease but who still experiences painful urination and a watery discharge is likely to have a form of NGU known as postgonococcal urethritis, or PGU. Its name, postgonococcal urethritis, implies that the condition appeared after the gonorrhea. Usually, however, the organisms responsible for the PGU were present in the urethra throughout the individual's bout of gonorrhea. As the incubation period for NGU is longer than that of gonorrhea, its symptoms may not have appeared until after the gonorrhea had been cured. The PGU was not cured along with the gonorrhea if penicillin or spectinomycin were used as the treatment. These medications are not effective against PGU. However, if tetracycline is used to treat the gonorrhea, PGU will not occur.

DIAGNOSIS

A patient who complains of a burning sensation upon urination as well as a urethral discharge will generally be tested for gonorrhea by a physician. If the tests indicate that gonorrhea is not present, then the doctor will usually assume that the patient is suffering from NGU.

In addition, a test to detect *Chlamydia trachomatis* in the urethral discharge should be performed.

TREATMENT

Antibiotics are usually prescribed to treat NGU. Several drugs have been found to be effective in combating NGU. The most commonly prescribed medication is tetracycline. Erythromycin is also used.

The majority of cases are cured within seven days. In treating nongonococcal urethritis, it is essential to take the full dosage of medication prescribed for the entire period indicated. The symptoms may disappear before the infection is fully cured, and if the medication is discontinued at this point, the infection may return in full force. During the course of the treatment, alcohol should be avoided, as it may further irritate the urethra.

All sexual contacts of the infected individual should be notified and receive treatment immediately. This is essential in order to prevent reinfection. Treatment for women is as important as it is for men since complications of NGU are more common in women than men.

Women are capable of unknowingly carrying and transmitting the organisms that produce NGU. These organisms in pregnant women may cause eye infections in newborn infants. If the NGU transmitted to a male partner is caused by *Chlamydia trachomatis,* the long-term effects may be devastating to the female as this organism can also cause PID (see page 71).

Other complications which may result from untreated NGU are epididymitis (see page 87), Reiter's syndrome, sterility, and proctitis, an inflammation of the rectum.

SEXUALLY
TRANSMITTED
DISEASES

CERVICITIS

Cervicitis is an inflammation of the cervix. It is believed to be caused by *Neisseria gonorrhoeae, Chlamydia trachomatis,* or herpes simplex virus.

The organisms which cause cervicitis are usually transmitted through sexual intercourse. However, pregnant women with cervicitis caused by the herpes virus may transmit the organisms to their infants during the birth process. Women with active herpes lesions at the time of delivery may consider delivery by cesarean section.

SYMPTOMS

Cervicitis has been a poorly understood infection since the cervix normally changes over the reproductive period and during the menstrual cycle. It may be difficult to distinguish between normal changes and changes resulting from infection. Also, symptoms are often absent. Many women with cervicitis have a completely normal cervix upon physical examination.

When symptoms are present, they are often not associated with cervicitis. Some women with cervicitis have a vaginal discharge that originates from the cervix. The discharge may contain mucus and pus. On occasion, this may be accompanied by a burning sensation upon urination. Some patients with cervicitis caused by herpes simplex virus have lower abdominal pain and genital lesions.

DIAGNOSIS

Since many women with cervicitis have normal cervixes, a physical examination is not adequate to identify the infection. Cervicitis must be confirmed by culture tests which isolate the disease-producing organisms.

TREATMENT

Tetracycline is most often used to treat an individual with cervicitis.

Treatment of cervicitis depends a great deal on the diagnosis of urethritis in male partners since urethritis has symptoms more often than cervicitis. The organisms which cause urethritis in men are very often transmitted through sexual contact and cause asymptomatic cervicitis in women. In fact, *Chlamydia trachomatis*—one of the causes of cervicitis—is isolated from as many as half of the female partners of men with nongonococcal urethritis. Therefore, many physicians believe that female partners of men with urethritis should be treated for cervicitis even before confirming the diagnosis.

SEXUALLY
TRANSMITTED
DISEASES

VAGINAL INFECTIONS
Trichomoniasis, Yeast Infections, Bacterial Vaginosis

There are several kinds of vaginal infection; not all are caused by sexually transmitted diseases.

Perhaps the most obvious symptom of vaginal infection is the presence of an excessive vaginal discharge. A certain amount of vaginal discharge is normal; however, a discharge which is symptomatic of vaginal infection tends to be heavier, will often have a foul odor, and may cause itching. A discharge caused by a yeast infection is odorless.

Vaginal infection does not pose a serious threat to a woman's good health generally. However, at least one form, called bacterial vaginosis, may increase the risk of acquiring pelvic inflammatory disease. In addition, at times vaginal infection may be difficult to cure and it is not uncommon for women to suffer recurrences.

TRICHOMONIASIS
also known as trichomonas vaginitis or trich

Trichomoniasis is caused by a one-celled parasite called *Tricho-monas vaginalis*. It is a form of vaginal infection which is most commonly acquired by sexual contact. Although it is technically possible for an individual to contract trichomoniasis from a toilet seat or wash cloth, it is highly unlikely. It is difficult to know how widespread trichomoniasis is, since many of the women who have it show no symptoms. It is possible for an individual to unknowingly harbor the *Trichomonas* organisms for years.

SYMPTOMS

In an infected woman, changes within the vaginal environment may cause the symptoms to surface. The symptoms may appear for a few days and then vanish for months. At times, a vaginal discharge may be the only symptom present. The discharge is usually yellowish, but it may take on a greenish tint, or it may be white or gray as well. The discharge usually emits a foul odor. The vaginal area may itch, and there may be a burning sensation when urinating. In the majority of cases in which symptoms are exhibited, they will generally appear between four days and one month after the initial contact with an infected partner.

An examination by a physician may reveal a slender rim of yellowish discharge surrounding the cervix. The vagina walls may have reddened, and in very severe cases red dots may develop on the cervix as well as on the walls of the vagina.

Most men infected with *Trichomonas* do not develop any symptoms. However, some men may experience a burning sensation when urinating or following ejaculation. In addition, the tip of the penis may itch.

DIAGNOSIS

Many doctors may suspect trichomoniasis simply from the characteristic symptoms. However, the diagnosis must be confirmed by examining the vaginal discharge under a microscope. However, even microscopic examination will not guarantee an accurate diagnosis all the time. For difficult cases, a culture test is available.

Since the discharge usually carries an unpleasant odor, often women douche prior to being examined by their physician, and in doing so, they may rinse away a large number of the organisms. Therefore, it is important not to douche at least 24 hours before an examination for any genital problem.

TREATMENT

Trichomoniasis is treated with metronidazole. However, this drug may not be taken by everyone. It should not be administered to people who have certain blood diseases, an active disease of the central nervous system, or to women in the first three months of pregnancy.

To reduce the symptoms during the treatment period, it is best to keep the vulva area dry. It is advisable to wear cotton underpants rather than synthetic garments, as cotton fabrics tend to absorb moisture.

The sexual partner of the infected individual also must be treated with metronidazole to prevent reinfection. The person being treated for trichomoniasis should abstain from sexual intercourse until he or she is cured. The purpose of such restrictions is to prevent infected individuals or those in the process of being treated from reinfecting one another and then passing the disease back and forth.

* * *

YEAST INFECTIONS
also known as candidiasis or moniliasis

Yeast infections, which are caused by overgrowth of a fungus known as *Candida albicans,* are more annoying than they are dangerous to a woman's health. They are extremely common in women and are often stubbornly difficult to get rid of. Even after effective treatment, recurrences are common.

Although it is possible for a man to transmit a yeast infection to a woman, it is far more likely that the female will pass it on to the male. Yeast infections commonly occur when a woman is taking antibiotics for another infection, such as a urinary tract infection, because when the normally occurring bacteria are also killed by the antibiotic, the environment in the vagina changes and yeast growth is encouraged. Yeast infections are also common during times of hormonal change, such as during pregnancy or while taking oral contraceptives.

Many women normally have small amounts of yeast in the vagina, so the presence of yeast doesn't necessarily mean someone has a vaginal infection.

SYMPTOMS

Yeast infection symptoms may vary among different women, but itching and irritation are the most common symptoms. There may be little or no vaginal discharge.

The discharge, if present, is of a whitish hue sometimes with thick curds of a white substance that looks something like cottage cheese. It is usually heaviest just preceding and following a woman's menstrual period. Upon a physician's examination, the vagina may appear red and swollen, and particles from the discharge may cling to the vaginal walls and cervix.

In some cases in which the discharge is especially abundant, an itchy rash may develop on the outside genitals. The vulva may become swollen, irritated, and extremely tender. A general soreness may develop in the genital area, and sexual intercourse may become quite painful.

Men are less likely than women to be troubled by yeast infections. A male's genitals are external, while on the other hand, the warm moist climate of a woman's vagina is more conducive to the growth of these organisms. However, yeast infections in men can sometimes cause a rash in the genital area.

DIAGNOSIS

In many instances, a physician is able to suspect a yeast infection just from the symptoms. However, for a definite diagnosis it is best for the doctor to take a sample of the discharge to be examined under a microscope for positive identification. This is important, since at times a yeast infection may be present in the vagina along with other infections, and the symptoms may be somewhat camouflaged.

TREATMENT

There are several antifungal medications used to treat yeast infections. They are available in creams, tablets, and coated tampons.

* * *

BACTERIAL VAGINOSIS
also known as Haemophilus vaginitis or nonspecific vaginitis

Bacterial vaginosis is the most common form of vaginal infection. Previously, these infections were diagnosed as nonspecific vaginitis. However, medical research has revealed that many cases of vaginal infection which were regarded as "nonspecific" were in fact associated with an organism called *Gardnerella vaginalis* as well as other bacteria. The exact cause of bacterial vaginosis is uncertain; the condition occurs when several organisms, including *Gardnerella vaginalis,* grow to larger than normal numbers.

SYMPTOMS

A large proportion of the women who suffer from bacterial vaginosis do not exhibit any symptoms in the initial stages of the infection. However, if a symptom is noticed, it will most likely appear as a thin, gray-colored vaginal discharge which has a bad odor. At times an infected individual may experience an itching or burning sensation, but this is far less likely to occur with bacterial vaginosis than in some other forms of vaginal infection.

DIAGNOSIS

Most physicians can diagnose bacterial vaginosis by testing a sample of the discharge.

TREATMENT

Bacterial vaginosis is treated with metronidazole. As with other forms of vaginal infection, doctors recommend that during the treatment period infected individuals either abstain from having sexual intercourse or that males wear a condom.

SEXUALLY
TRANSMITTED
DISEASES

EPIDIDYMITIS

Epididymitis is an inflammation of the epididymis, the long cordlike structure located along the back of the testis. The most common type of epididymitis in young men is sexually transmitted epididymitis. It is usually caused by *Chlamydia trachomatis* or *Neisseria gonorrhoeae*. Epididymitis may result as a complication of urethral infection by one of these two bacteria, and is the male counterpart of PID in women. However, it is much less common than PID.

Acute epididymitis may result in the formation of abscesses and infertility.

SYMPTOMS
The most common symptom of epididymitis is painful swelling of the scrotum. Some individuals may experience painful urination and a urethral discharge.

DIAGNOSIS
A physician may suspect epididymitis through an evaluation of the symptoms along with an examination of the scrotum and

urethra. A culture of the urethral discharge to detect *C. tracho-matis* or *N. gonorrhoeae* is usually taken to confirm the diagnosis. Examination of urine specimens may also be helpful.

TREATMENT

Epididymitis is usually treated with tetracycline. Bed rest with elevation of the scrotum is recommended to reduce swelling and pain. Sexual partners of individuals with epididymitis should also be treated.

GLOSSARY

antibiotic—a medication chiefly used in the treatment of infectious diseases which inhibits the growth of bacteria and other microorganisms.

asymptomatic—exhibiting no sign of a contracted disease or illness.

bubo—greatly enlarged inflamed lymph nodes usually located in the groin, often associated with several sexually transmitted diseases.

cervix—the lower tip of the uterus, which extends and opens into the vagina.

chancre—an ulcer or sore with a hard base, usually located in the genital area, and which is most often associated with syphilis and chancroid.

culture—the growing of microorganisms in a controlled environment for medical purposes.

curette—a scoop-shaped surgical instrument used to scrape diseased tissue from body cavities such as the uterus.

douche—a jet or current of water applied to the vagina for medicinal or hygienic purposes.

ejaculation—the process of discharging semen by the reproductive organs of the male.

fallopian tube—one of a pair of ducts opening at one end into the uterus and at the other end into the peritoneal cavity over the ovary.

foreskin—the fold of skin which covers the head of the penis or clitoris.

gynecologist—a doctor who specializes in gynecology, the area of medical science which is involved with the functions and diseases of women, especially regarding the reproductive organs.

incubation period—the time between contracting a disease and the appearance of symptoms.

inflammation—swelling, redness, pain, and tenderness, most often as a reaction of bodily tissues to injurious agents.

labia—the folds of skin and mucous membrane of the external genitalia or vulva surrounding the entrance of the vagina.

lesion—any injurious or abnormal change in a localized area of tissue, such as a blister, chancre, sore, etc.

mucous membrane—a lubricating membrane which lines an internal surface.

pap smear—a procedure or test for women used primarily to detect cancerous or precancerous cells in the cervix.

scrotum—the pouch of skin covering the male reproductive glands.

semen—the sperm-containing fluid of males.

sitz bath—the immersion of the thighs and hips in warm water as part of a therapeutic treatment.

testis (testes, pl)—one of two reproductive glands located in the cavity of the scrotum.

urethra—the tube running from the urinary bladder to the exterior, in men both urine and semen travel through the urethra.

vulva—the external genitalia of a female.

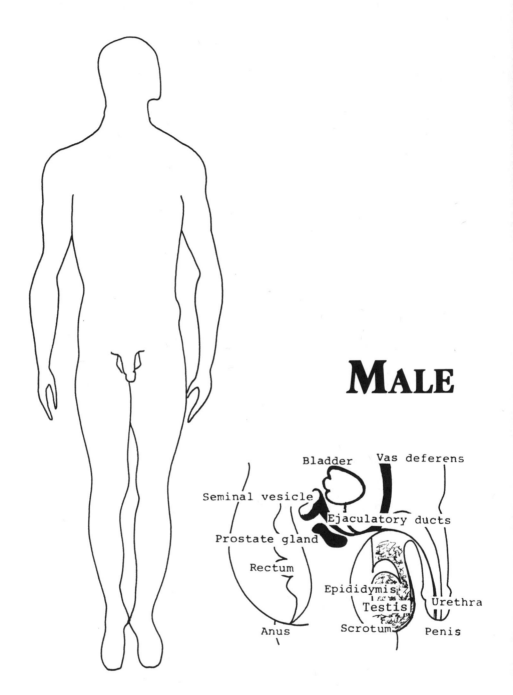

MALE

Bladder

Vas deferens

Seminal vesicle

Ejaculatory ducts

Prostate gland

Rectum

Epididymis

Urethra

Testis

Anus

Scrotum

Penis

FEMALE

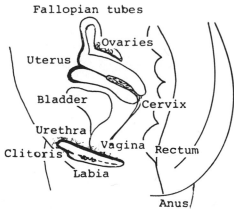

Fallopian tubes

Ovaries

Uterus

Bladder

Cervix

Urethra

Clitoris

Vagina

Rectum

Labia

Anus

FURTHER READING

Balis, Andrea. *What Are You Using: A Birth Control Guide for Teenagers.* Fayetteville, New York: Ed-U Press, 1981.

Barlow, David. *Sexually Transmitted Diseases: The Facts.* New York: Oxford University Press, 1981.

Bell, Ruth, et. al. *Changing Bodies, Changing Lives: A Book for Teens on Sex & Relationships.* New York: Random, 1981.

Burgess-Kohn, Jane. *Straight Talk About Love and Sex for Teenagers.* Boston: Beacon Press, 1979.

Chase, Allan. *The Truth About STD: The Old Ones—Herpes & Other New Ones—the Primary Causes—the Available Cures.* New York: Morrow, 1983.

Edwards, George J. *Facts About Syphilis and Gonorrhea.* Palo Alto, California: Learning Line, 1972.

Gale, Jay. *A Young Man's Guide to Sex.* New York: Holt, Rinehart and Winston, 1984.

Gordon, Sol. *Facts About STD—Sexually Transmitted Diseases.* Fayetteville, New York: Ed-U Press, 1983.

Hyde, Margaret O. *VD: The Silent Epidemic.* Second Edition. New York: McGraw-Hill, 1982.

Johnson, Eric. *Love and Sex in Plain Language.* Revised Edition. New York: Harper & Row, 1985.

Llewellyn-Jones, Derek. *Herpes, AIDS, & Other Sexually Transmitted Diseases.* Winchester, Massachusetts: Faber & Faber, 1985.

McGuire, Paula. *It Won't Happen to Me: Teenagers Talk About Pregnancy.* New York: Delacorte, 1983.

Madaras, Lynda, and Madaras, Area. *What's Happening to My Body? A Growing-Up Guide for Mothers and Daughters.* New York: Newmarket, 1983.

Nourse, Alan E. *Herpes.* New York: Franklin Watts, 1985.

Redfern, Paul. *The Love Diseases.* Secaucus, New Jersey: Citadel Press, 1981.

Richards, Arlene K., and Willis, Irene. *What to Do If You or Someone You Know is 18 & Pregnant.* New York: Lothrop, 1983.

Zinner, Stephen. *STD: Sexually Transmitted Diseases.* New York. Summit Books, 1985.

INDEX

PPNG (penicillinase-producing
  N. gonorrhoeae), 22
pregnancy
  herpes and, 40-41
  syphilis and, 32-33
pubic lice, 54-56
public health department, report-
    ing of sexually transmitted
    disease to, 13

R
rectal herpes, 38-39

S
salpingitis, 71-75. *See also* pelvic
    inflammatory disease (PID)
scabies, 56-57
Scarcoptes scabiei, 56-57
sexually transmitted disease, 7-14
  contraceptive techniques and,
    7-8
  discharge in, 9
  increase in, 7
  medical examinations in, 10-13
    clinic or public health depart-
      ment for, 12
    family physician and, 11
    of minors, 12-13
    Planned Parenthood clinic in,
      12
    VD National Hotline and, 12
    yearly testing in, 11
  odor as sign of, 9
  prevention of, 8-10
    condoms in, 10
    partner's health status in, 8-9
    urination in, 10
    washing hands and genitals in,
      10
  public health department
    reporting of, 13
    sexual mores and, 7

shigellosis, 64-65
soft chancre, 50-51
syphilis, 29-34
  chancre in, 29-30
  diagnosis of, 33
  gumma in, 31-32
  latent, 31
  pregnancy and, 32-33
  primary, 29-30
  secondary, 30-31
  symptoms of, 29-32
  tertiary or late, 31-32
  treatment of, 33-34

T
Treponema pallidum, 29
"trich." *See* trichomoniasis
Trichomonas vaginalis, 81-83
trichomoniasis, 81-83

U
Ureaplasma urealyticum, 63
urethritis. *See* nongonococcal
    urethritis
urination, in prevention of sexually
    transmitted disease, 10

V
vaginal infection, 81-86
vaginitis, nonspecific, 85-86
vaginosis, bacterial, 85-86
VD National Hotline, 12
venereal warts, 42-44

W
warts
  anal, 43
  genital or venereal, 42-44

Y
yeast infections, 83-85